How Things Change

How
Things
Change
by Ronnie Barnes

Dedicated chiefly to my family: Estrella, Josiah, and Claire...
the joys of my heart and the crown of my life.

Dedicated to my mom, dad, and all of my family in Sumter, SC, and each of my
five amazing sisters.

Dedicated to my friends who encouraged me over the past two years to put my
poetry into print.

Dedicated also to all of my students, both in high school and college. There is no
greater delight than to see you grow, and grow into God's direction for your life.

Dedicated to my church family who allow me the time for what my various writing
projects demand.

This collection of poems explores how things are and how they
change — how society and its subjects change as they interact with
each other and themselves. Strong themes of existential curiosity
and wall-testing, personal power to effect change, and the human
instinct to adapt oneself to life's firm bounds are present
throughout, along with the occasional respite of nostalgic longing
that ultimately resolves to both present action and future hope.

ISBN: 979-8-9873028-0-4

Printed by Book Mobile
Minneapolis, MN
www.BookMobile.com

Published by Altamont Media Publishing
Laurens, South Carolina
www.AltamontMedia.net

Titles:	**Coolvetica**
Body Text:	TW Cen MT

Cover Art:	"How Things Change" by Ronnie Barnes
	digital, 2022

Contents

Contents

3 Bonus Poems from Other Collections

Rare Creatures of the Deep

This poem is featured in **"Under the Sun"**, a collection of poems whose subject matter is nature, and from every vantage and angle. The journey begins offshore before progressing to a beach front and into the woods. It is a loosely linear journey, but certainly one with plenty of natural interest and charged imagery to entertain on the way. I included this poem here for my father, Ronnie W Barnes Sr, who really enjoyed it.

The Master Piece

This poem is featured in **"Messages"**, a collection whose universal aim is to stimulate spiritual contemplation in the follower of Jesus Christ. They are heavy with doctrinal musings, thoroughly concerned with morality and character and a variety of theological matters, and ready with commensurate exhortations.

Black and White Days

This poem is featured in **"Misfits"**, a collection of poetic B-sides that were too distinct to include in other collections, but also demanded their inclusion somewhere. After a while of seeing this happen, they banded together to become a collection unto themselves!

Part 1:
The Problem
Defined and
Resolved

Hard Now to Find

No longer a common thing to find
Buried amidst a million new clean lines
All things refreshed, refined, or replaced
To accommodate a quickly quickening pace.

No longer a common thing to find
Something slow-but-stable in time
The product of a simpler, sturdier day
The fruit of the warmth of well-worn ways.

Efficiency now the rule under which all new things endure
Or be cast off to be trampled to be pulverized to be blown
By hot-and-hard winds that won't relent
Until what is new is all that is left
Until all that's old is broke and spent.

And it's hard also now to find
Another soul who could sympathize with the tone of this whine
"It all seems so unwise to reflect on what's gone...
And have in your hand no plan to resolve...
Your dubious gripe about the tone of this time."

And what could one say, when what's said seems so true?
Is the problem of progress just that it's always too soon?
Or is there something true lost in the shuffle to renew?
Or is it all fear, and all threat — defense against the imminent next?

Irony abounds, and it's hard now to find a reason to resist what now pours so swift...
And harder still to resign to the comfort of what's quickly fading away. All those fears, so rightly discerned, vacating like washing tides on a shore.
And sooner still to return and remind me again of their validated presence at days' end.

Tensions as tight as the times that I have seen and also now see; like an out-of-tune guitar, with its tuner frantically, turning and hearing and tuning again to make the right sound come out in the end.

But the knobs keep resetting when the tuner moves on — a shifting sea with no boat to sit on, and no compass to guide to a rested shore when day is done.

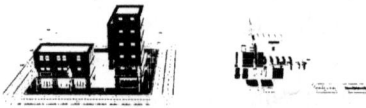

Paradise: Lost and Found

LOST

Formed, fitted, and framed to perfection — a clear image of God.
Set amid a garden paradise, far beyond what we could comprehend.
Man, so created and so placed, to fill purpose and commune with Creator, face to face.
There was no knowledge but of God — no awareness of good and evil, no knowledge of an enemy beyond those outer gates.

How far did it stretch?
How did it all seem?
How tall were its trees?
How clear were its streams?

However many questions we might pile up high, one thing remains clear, we must keep it in mind:
"If man made it, it will vanish. If man touched it, it will perish."
There's just no way around it; it must be seen as being true. It is the knowledge gate leading to wisdom, for those who would make it through.

None of it makes sense apart from the way that it actually happened. It frames it on the front end, and declares what should be like after. A set of bookends stretched way over the line of time. Mirror it completely to see how it ends.

Firstly, of a paradise formed by God, then invaded and corrupted; finally, of a world deformed and infested, then restructured to a warped paradise, mocking God.

But all things will be made new by the One who builds without human hand that would make it fail. And we're not there yet.

For now, we have the problem of the ages, with wars and treachery from the highest places: plotting plans of evil to be

11

carried out; creating catastrophes all around to coax fear; fomenting division between the people to destroy them all.

(If only there were a coat for the coax, to somehow weather well the rain-down from hell. There is.)

FOUND

Cleansed and sharpened and all around brightened.

Light streams and diffuses across large patches of low-riding clear-fog causing brilliant displays of colorflows and across beautiful horizons.

Wind so warm and mild and welcoming, and there's no real reason to be found to do anything other than just hang around.

Life meant for living, an apple under a tree, leisurely chomp and chew under cool shade's dew, nowhere else to be.

And none of it all alone, what's a house without being a home? People like me as far as new eye can see — all in godly love and true peace and harmony; all in the state of Paradise, the place to be.

—

And after all of this to find, all that was just a paradise in the mind — made no bearing on what would be, no real echo in eternity.

Nevertheless, found going in the right direction, upward in hope, sincere in affection, all toward God.

Though a mind could scarcely be found to hold true vision of what is to come, there is at the seed of every yearning heart a blueprint of eternal home.

There is a proper place for pondering on that space, to uncover
something that might just
give itself up to sincerest eye; that is to say, not to one whose
pious intention proceeds from selfish pride. (Vanity would dare to
spy out to where it has no right, under guise of wanting light.)

—

I figure time smiles kindly on a God-softened soul, who's arrived
to a place of resignation before its almighty Creator and King.

And I can be sure of at least that much concerning Paradise.

Good Things Come

Part 1

Part of the time of this life is to sow
And yet another is found in the grow
In all of it found, yeah, it's plain to see:

"The good things come to those who try...
It won't ever come to those who deny...
The importance of self and the work of the day...
The good things that come are the self-given pay."

It's not lost on me that it's mostly that way
But exceptions abound, can be seen every day
Where the good reap what's bad, from the good thing they've sown
And the bad rejoice greatly, though their works can't be shown

But God is not mocked, and He never will be
Whatever a man sows, it is that he will reap
And we should rejoice for the great Gift He has given
Yes, and through Jesus Christ, all these concepts are lifted.

To an exalted and pure new place.

Part 2

Yeah, there are many who try to defy
The logic of order of Creation on High
And feign to pretend to assign out the blame
Accuse always some other — a full lack of shame
For all of the bad things that have come

And it's an evil under the sun, it must be
To see such wrong tears to fall down so free
And yet still, to see others gather for their comfort
All abandon their fallowed fields for one another
And return only again to sit and resign
And lament the good thing that won't come in their time.

But the surprise of it all is when the moment fades
Yet the lights remain on still another day
And the good thing comes to those who fainted
On fallow ground, where they lay (another evil under the sun)

Ever effusive of the evil around
As the good thing nurtures their evil sound
And the branch where they sit upon high in the sky
Begins to creak and to crack, under the weight of what they lack

Yeah, it groans for the weight of the evil there-on
And the petty complaints of the wicked who fawn
For the firm ground below, though they climbed in the tree.
Ever insistent for the heights they would see
And they'll soon meet the ground; there, they'll soon be.

And for now, they're well-nourished in their great self-deceit
Self-insisted good fortune that's fulfilled their instinct
Willing good things to be for them in their selfish malaise
Still regretting the evil of their self-made days.
The good things that could come to such a sollowful soul
Is nothing less than the fruit of their work
Which is nothing more than nothing at all
A hollow harvest, comforted in deceit
The good things that come is the end of some things
The end of the messenger with no solution to bring.
The time of their life is in judging what's sown
Not knowing what's known
Not finding their home
Just willing to roam
Not planting to sow
Not reaping what's grown
All just weeds, and so shallow.

Part 3

And on the other end is something harder to see
When the ones who are good are found sowing good seed
And their labors are known both in Heaven and earth.
And they feed on the fruit of the strength of their work

Another evil under the sun, it must be:
To see when the crops are stolen by thieves
Or the equipment burned asunder
Or the soil be turned sour under
Or the harvest never come for their wait

The diligent hand who finds nothing but sand
Passing through calloused hands
And mingled with tears

Such injustice cannot stand.
Earth itself will contort in revolt
To right such a wrong displayed.
In their time, all will be repaid.

They're no stranger to hot days
And no stranger to cold nights
And protecting what they've invested
And engaging fully what is right.

And though some bad thing befall them
And though it happen seven times...

They will rise again
righteous till the end.
God not ashamed to be called their Friend.
Truly His help will find them in the end.
Those who sew in tears will finally win
And reap with joy the good things to come.

Part 4

And among all the movements on the spectrum
of work and rights, and wrongs and fights
We find a curious line upward, between it all
That elevates discussion to its ultimate plane
Where there can be no further talk of ought, or of blame, or of
shame.

Where the first sowing is pre-reckoned, and the harvest made
free to all
Who would believe in the name of the only begotten Son of God,
Jesus Christ.
Whose death paid the way, the first-fruit from the grave —
ascended, that all might walk their way back to the Father in
Heaven above.

And the great gift bestowed doesn't speak like the previous
And it cannot abide by the logic so shown
As it relies on the principle of 'freely given'
And since, freely given, then freely owned
To be handled with great care

The foundations raised high above mortal planes of toil and
trouble
and problems of soil or an enemy's foil can't raze what's been
built to rubble.

God is not mocked, and everyone shall reap, the fruit of the work
they have done will be seen
And whether it be of wood or hay or chaff, not to last
Or if it be of silver or gold, of most refined metals, through the
fire have passed

The name of the One who made it all come to pass
Will be elevated above all — the author of the new world —
clothed in righteousness
Sown all in tears, but reaping then in resplendent joy, altogether

18

Those who have sown just to reap full despair, thinking justice was gone, will be seen as an heir
To a kingdom so full of what all they have sown.
"Enter into the joy of your Master", the sweetest sound to be known...

And finally see all the good things come.

How Things Change

Part 1: The Circle Shrinks

At the corruption of the greater, when the better version — more
robust and senior and ornamented and skillfully made — is of
necessity replaced with the junior, which has no room for fancy,
full, or fanciful, but is limited in all its reach and potencies to
restrain a less deserving subject coursing its paths beneath.

Like a tornado, so formed to ravage its occasion for birth, or a
cancer that grows in a body to kill.
A clean slate, like after a storm, but not without its vast evidence
of destruction and unrecoverable loss.
Civilizations fall and evidence of their glory is scarcely
recovered, and even those trinkets are uncovered with great
difficulty, fractured as they are.

If there is anything worth being remembered, it fails the test to be
reconciled to a new and lesser context — a relic out of time and
a fragile foreigner, scarcely retained in its new and hostile
terrain.
Scraps from a greater age in ways we could never understand
— in ways they put it all together to make it work within their
hand. Basic from our vantage yet diverged to greater depths; on
the one hand lacking, and on the other hand higher than we've
felt.

"So simple," they say, "yet refined in its display."
"What function might it perform? For what application was it
formed?"
The luxury of such questions such a contrast to the violence where
all was lost.
And the scraps that are now found, are as pebbles under the
ground.

Part 2: The Flesh Self-Corrupts

Eyes turned now toward man, and the root of such riot that abounded to rebellion preceding the breakdown of all things. Abundance of bread and wine, cheap thrills all around, lazy days, endless vain praise, a 'total entertainment future', as they now even dare to say.

It's never understood until too late, that the late-blooming flower is fuel for its own fate.
Thoroughly nourished, set to grow, rise, and bloom — fig tree in its season, but no evidence of fruit. So, set to be cursed for its dereliction of life, and its laze under haze, and its love lost for light.

Daring to think in softest corner of its darkening heart, that the moons soft beams might prove a better start. They reckon, "From there, we can find a fresh start."

So, it seems to be that inversion has become the sacred key, set down now to make us free, from every whim of the tyranny of soft winds blowing our way, sent to stoke a flame to keep darkness at bay. "It speaks against us!", they now even dare to say.
Thoroughly nourished, stomach turned sour by the sun setting too soon. One hates to leave, but there's no reason to be found to wait another moon.

Setting sun alights the sky, like a burnt offering, only glorious now as it dies.

Part 3: Enlightenment Interposed

Seeing through such a ruptured veil, to find there's not much flowing there like once was, can leave one in the depths of despair, and apprehension of what's yet to come.

A world alight with violence, fools as fodder for a thirsty fire. There is no claim for such a man who lives as wild on softened land, who gates-off peace, and chops his way through already broken alleys and treacherous ways.
Restless and snarling and all-around gnarly, vicious and poised to sniff a faint scent of blood, then to attach and attack.
Why does such a beastly form merit intervention of divine warmth, or celestial comfort, or merciful remediation?
Trained in dark rays, skilled in evil ways, prone to invent new ways to go wrong.

And somehow, we still find good news, and directly aimed at such a world of violence.

Part 4: Merits Toward a Future World

In full height of skill and full depth of reach, He bathes the world in what it needs.
And cleanses with fire the violent and liar and purifies all who would bow at His feet.
To somehow install a New Module within, that can forestall all the rot, and wipe away sin.
And fit the unfit for a better world to be made — a better way to be paved, upward and away from all that must be left behind.
To say it is one thing, and to see it is another; and to believe it and adopt it is the only way He's covered as fee for what He would give fully to the soul who would be made free.

And all of this designed from the start, even before the line was crossed. And even before the stain was set, there was already a solution in His mind to be set into play, to make the ink be wiped away before it bites into the page.

Not a rewind, nor a deface — not a bruised reed would He even need to break.

He kept all things in proper place, with proper pace, so skillfully molding and moving the hearts of prophets of old, and also kings and princes and common folk, and all of that across the great line of time.

To ultimately reveal the fulness of His design, for all to see and rejoice on that day, when all dark panels will be peeled away.

And as a tapestry turned from its back to its front, the unveiling of what's new will be a Magnificent One.

As He finally reveals something greater than all — even greater than all that we lost in the fall — to the full assembly of all who had believed that what they had left behind was less than what was to come; and what they had suffered was not a vain run; and that all they had lost is now all found in Him — the great King of all Kings, Jesus Christ, God's own Son.

Growing in its Direction

Straining to see the light: how it plays on moving and growing things; how it constrains and molds and forms as it pings and punctures and performs all of its easy wonders on a human soul. Such a strain, like I said, for light-glazed eyes to see its soft efforts and realize how time marches on and things grow as they should, and everything winds around and comes back as good as it first started, only slightly lifted upward and matured, toward its proper place of staity.

Every plant formed of its own seed, and every human the same, it seems.
And what a wild thing it is, I guess, that the light that so forms a soul can also demand so much for the inquirer of the method; an eye on the process can make one blind.

Better maybe to just see, than to see how it works?
To know and be found impotent, or to be simple but in full vigor of life?

Better to let the light use you and do its things to you, than to dare to stand apart and appraise the work. Maybe.

Better to be as the clay on the wheel, not a pot on a shelf — ready to be formed, rather than ready to tell the potter how to turn or throw.

And as the light recedes and darkness creeps, the waning eye could maybe finally see the mysteries I've found — maybe the thing about things growing in their own direction; maybe something else. Lots of mysteries out there, seeming so simple on the surface, but running so deep underneath.

But there's just nothing like getting an eye full of something so elegant, well-formed, and simple — the way God made everything, really. But to see one thing moving and doing all its functions... it's just something else.

Like not every parable can be fit into one, or every song sung at once. A properly discerned piece of the larger machine, just sitting there to be seen, turned, admired.
Maybe I'm the pot, already done; that's why I'm willing to reflect.
Maybe I'm the clay, still waiting to be spun. I wouldn't be the only one.

I know I'm no potter; that's the Lord's work, after all — making things grow in their direction.

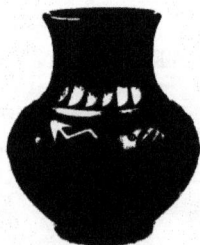

Part 2:
The Matters
Explored and
Accepted

An Open Door

Placed before me in quiet constraints
Movement all within, above, and around me pulls
In the valley of decision, set high above it all
And I've already chosen, it would seem
Which door that I will call
The direction I will fall.

An open door — certainly the choice was real
Though in the moment, all instinct and feel.
The open door, I saw from long ago
And saw the day approaching, where I would have to know
Which one I would choose
So, I choose
Deep in my history, in the distant haze of past days
All so open and clear to me now
On the other side
The road I chose so long ago
Fit me well future.

A Certain Kind of Smile

Turnings - like valleys and mountain tops – come.
But at every turning, not everything is saved.
Some things get left behind, lost in the fray.
Some things get promoted, yeah, but some left behind.
Some things sweet, some are sour, they all have their time.

But to the point I want to make:
the value of what's sometimes not saved
A certain kind of smile, let me try to describe.
Can no longer be found in the time that we find:

Easy, and confident, sure and resolved.
Light and assured of the time where it lives.
Eager to hope for more of what it gives.

A certain kind of smile can't be worn in this time.
It's out of design.
There's no occasion to find
this archaic smile
this age left behind.

In favor of a certain kind of dread
More favorable to what must lie ahead
A certain kind of smile has no place in such land.

Tough Times Don't Last

Sittin' cold and alone, all wrapped up at home
Feelin' it's all gonna end, and that you don't have a friend

Memories of better days, haunt troubled mind
And there's no pattern to discern on this design.
All this happenin' without reason or rhyme.
Wonderin' when it'll turn, when it'll be your time.

Tough times don't last
Can't last o'er the day
All this trouble that's piled up
Must soon be on its way

I'm sittin' here waitin' for the tides to pull back
For the setting sun to wash my cares away
Into a sea of forgetfulness where they can stay
The cool moon console me to a new day.

Tough times don't last
Can't carry o'er settled horizon
All my sorrows that have weighed me
Will soon be found waning, on God's scales.

I'm sittin' here tryin' to keep my tears to myself
But the moisture escapes me, touches floor of my cell
And the prison bars, through them I see free stars
Going on their way, touching cool air on their way
Not bound like me to stay.

And that will be me one day.

Gate to Nowhere

Built a gate in an open field.
Left it there and went away.
Thought nothin' else, till the whole world grew one day.
And now the gate is an entryway.

I was called a fool, well, it was just a statement
of how life can feel so tight but also vacant.
I built a fixture way out on open land, where no one was, and
nothing could be found.

A certain joy, a certain charm is what I sought
to build a think where no one had ever thought.
A monument to my hope for better days, where I could have a
hand in how it all would play.

It's all so tight, so wrapped and bound; I can't be alone here with
what I've found.
A gate to nowhere, it seems, can someday become
on a road to somewhere, built by someone.

A Lone, Soon-Worn Path

It's always up, always ahead
The next platform above my head
The last step lost, no longer new
The next way forward, hard to do

The new thing must come
I must leave behind
Everything old: of comfort, of time

The way must be blazed
And the trail be made new
For those who would follow
To do what I do

I must not remember
Nor regard, nor opine
The treasures I found
I must leave behind

Those who would come
And walk in my way
Must have a sure foot
And be blessed when they stay

Some will travel long
Some will camp out
Some will keep going
Some will clock out

Some will endure, carry long past my way
Some will go further, new trails to blaze.

The Woven Path

I went to the place where it is broken.
I went to the edge of where I can be.
And I gazed at it with great certainty.

"This is my bound...
Right here, I have found...
The place that I'm locked...
No other land to be found."

The edge, I sought out with such a privileged step, I know.
Not wandering known paths, but down dark paths I rode.
I rode till I've found the only place I can't be.
And I set up a camp for a pity party.

And such a vain thing to want just what you can't know.
And to only lament the thing that you can't hold.
And yet here I sit, blank gaze glazed on my face.
Not feeling camps fire, not seeing its flame.

Not wandering any longer down no paths I've known
Just camped in strange places, close to greater unknowns.
Living out on the edge, no it ain't for everyone.
And it also isn't for me, but right here I still run.

Though I'm looking to rise, it's my reason to be.
And I look in the skies, peel back layers to see.
All the wires that run long, all here to and fro.
All the connections I'm wanting, so I can finally go...

To the new places I've found, alighted by my foot's path.
The then dark places now shown, illuminated at last.
Then-woven paths untangled as I find a new place to pass.

I Knew of a Man

I knew of a man who tucked himself deep into the past; for the horror of the present, he chose to live for what could never last. And he prayed it would never pass, what had already faded so fast.

And his pining was a surge, was a great depth of an urge. Restless he cried into the past, so bound and tied as it was. And yet none of it could ever make room for a man to reside.

But I knew of this man who dared to defy the winds and the currents that come from on high, whose wistfulness mingled with woe turned his whole ship from shore, and off to hazy horizons filled with rare promises of unsure reward.

He must've caught a glimpse of something so true, whose beauty fascinated him to a place so sure, that no meager mouth could walk him back, or talk him down, or make his mind release the thing he dared to try to grasp.

He empowered it all by faith, claiming if he would but ask, that He would deliver, and that if he would but knock, then He would surely open for him to enter.

And such a man — so set apart, so willing to depart — declares himself that he was made for a world that no longer exists, or perhaps never did, or perhaps someday will.

Yet in his depth of heart he knows it was at the very least an ember of eternity sparking to a blaze in his mind, aimed to ignite a proper desire to find his way to distant shores foretold, to a place where beauty never ceases, and God's glory unfolds constant as it increases.

By faith, Abraham left to live in the land of promise. Like in a foreign land, he lived in tents with Isaac and Jacob — heirs with him of the same promise — because he was looking for the city whose foundations were designed and built by God.

By faith also, Sarah received the ability to conceive, though she was beyond childbearing years, because she considered him to be faithful who had made the promise.

Therefore, from one man — and him as good as dead — descendants were born as many as the stars of heaven and as many as the innumerable grains of sand by the seashore.

These all died in faith, having not received the things promised, but only seeing and greeting them from afar, confessing themselves to be strangers and exiles on the earth.

And people who speak like this make it clear that they are seeking a new homeland. If they had been thinking of the land from which they had departed, they would have taken the opportunity to return to it. But as it is, they show that they desire a better country, that is, a heavenly one. Therefore, God is not ashamed to be called their God, for he has prepared a city for them.

— The Epistle to the Hebrews
Chapter 11:9-16
proprietary translation

Well-Set in the Past

A fixture suspended in haze of lost days
In the mire of the mirror of forgotten ways
A stirring, desire, longing, pining I feel
To somehow get back there to that place

It's so unreal, so unfair to resign
To a place with no friction, no doors, no design
It's all set and staid, frozen, never to move
Never to make any new room, for a foreigner's feign

Quit trying, quit prying, leave it all, let it be.
The voices, they just won't quit saying to me
It's all well-set, reckoned, sealed in the past
Nothing, man, will last
It all wraps up so fast

Get your head up with the fresh air of what's here
There's time to make new things that later eyes can cheer
And pine for also, for all the new things adorned
On time's certain tapestry, yet to be worn.

Blind Corners

Feeling my way to find a rare diamond in the mine.
Rushing around, can't ever help it, no can't seem to make it slow.
To find a blind corner in a world so alive — so conscious, alert,
and ready to strike.
No place for a free man to find... lay around for a while, there's
no place to hide.
Gotta crawl out, can't stay in the mine for all time.

Blistering sun, calling out for someone, making everyone run for
cover.
Cover of shade, hide me in your deep grays, and shift me over to
a blind corner, where there's an oasis built for needed slumber.
Heavy days of endless rays suck the soul and the life.
Gotta make it all right, somehow.
If I can somehow make it to a blind corner for a while.

There's more to say about all that, but it pales to compare to the
higher and nobler desire this all points to so surely: not a blind
corner for shade from what would invade, but an eternal respite
— delivered into an open Heaven.

Open Heaven, no need to hide from any danger, it's all outside.
Light, not for burn but for warmth surging deep to cleanse and
renew; bring life to burnt and desiccated places.

No need to hide.
No further need for a blind corner at all.

Distant Lands Now Fading

I can see it so clear as I pull up to park
And the lines are already blending with broken pavement
Vestiges of a time gone by, barely hanging on.
Quickly moving on.
But for now, here I am.
Defiant of the unrelenting march of time
And of progress, which is vain, prone to forget every name
And every warm memory transcribed upon the line of time

And inside still warm, as I open the door
And move through familiar halls that hug me in mutual embrace
And the dream subsists so strong on the pleasant memory of what
I long
The warmth of family whole, and in one place.
Not divided by the brittle blows of foes and foibles
(and all of that from years past!)
Not separated by the distance of lands, so persistent in the
present.
Not fractioned in obstinate social bubbles so thick.
But whole. And warm. And like that distant land now fading
Called the past.
Or at least all I can recall of it.

A Small Way Back

A small way back I spotted
Out the corner of my very concerned eye.

Even you said you didn't know
How we could make it back
To more even times

I thought it was all lost and gone
Destitute, a lost cause
Goodbye.

And like an apparition
It appeared
As if to say "I've been here all along."

Like a red carpet it unrolled
Ready to pave my feet on its way

A small way back
Yeah, it is better than none.
I see it, can you see it
We've no space of time
No time to rewind
Just time back to run

Coming Home from Another Way

It's about time to find it again
And go to where from I was sent.
Finally making the journey back home
But from a very different place.
Coming back home from another way.
And the view as foreign to me
As the feeling inside that I carry
As the winding thin road I can see.

The journey still a theory, all mapped out inside my head.
Just splotches of blanks between both the X.
Not even ready to ask what is next.
Not even in my shoe to take my first steps.

But I'm ready, and weary, and ready to go.
Just looking for a sign to walk out the door.
Turn my back on the things that grabbed and refused to let go.
Thankful enough to agree to let go
To come home from another way.

Present Lands Now Shifting

And the jarring sudden shock
The crashing and its sound
Resound deep in my soul
To remind me of what's happening now,
Of present lands now shifting
(Not to even speak of what was, and is now leaving!)
How the present has lost its vital source
To construct in the moment some special fount
And produce that good and special sauce
That coats the memories for harsher days ahead.

"It's all gone!" in dismal dawn I proclaim
As if the sky were falling, and there's no time to blame.
The sky is stirring.
The hour is going.
The pot is boiling.
The alarm is blaring.

And I am now awake.
And it was all just a dream.
But a dream of a time that I loved. And that I love.
And I miss it. Because it can never happen again.
But the dream will keep it alive for me still, fresh for another day.

You Can't Go Home

Hollowed out walls, now only memories of etched memories
Transcribed to the line just to be lost to all time
And you can't make it back to what you would never forget
But what we always forget is so sad
That we are forgotten to the places that so formed us.

You can't go home, though you see it and it's there
You're long gone, can't quite touch what is always moving away
Though in vain you may try to stay, and make it stay, it will only
fade.

Oh, but don't be too heart-broken, too down-trodden, too lost for
this all.
It was likely not as good as you recall.
In the finest mist of distant memories, rewarmed.
Scarce is the memory that gives its reward.
Often is the memory to echo back harm.

Only the pining for what is gone fuels the drive to be back home
And the dread of what has come, to drive you from your current
place.
Back to the safest space of where you can never stay.

Like I said, it's always drifting away.
And even faster as you try to bend it back to your way.
Like the pendulum, it will soon be more distant than before.

So go home to where you came from, seeking warmth from what
was old and fading.
Go home to what you've lived in, and find your solace through
present vision.
And don't be bothered by what could never stay.
Let it speak to you a different way.
Let it guide you, as if to say, "this old thing brought you to now.
Don't look back, there's nothing left; it's hollowed out."

Part 3: The Futures Possible and Inevitable

What Happens Next

On tangents weird and twisted, taut.
Where normal lines are blurred or cut.
The path we knew, now distant thrown
Where can we go, in times unknown.

"What Happens Next?" A common ask.
How can we fit ourselves to task?
The times are new, but good? Untrue.
So what is it that we should do.

"What Happens Next?" In foreign field.
Far from the home, with broken wheel.
And setting sun, won't bring us 'round.
Can't comfort sleep, can't find us found.

"What Happens Next?" Well, no one knows.
Right! No one lives who could **ever** know.
But high above, exists the One
In whose great hand spins everyone.

And what happens next, is plain to see.
When you look to the One who made it be.

Fixed eyes can gaze with surest calm...
and surest calm can warm each one...
as each one moves in sudden peace...
and peace can lull restless heart to sleep...
to sleep and find the deepest rest...
and rest, wake refreshed, in cleansing breath.

The new day dawns, and strength is found.
For the better days, put feet to ground.

Put hand to plow! / Put heart to sing!
Put joy to speak! / And hope to ring!

"What happens next?"
No more despairing of life
But in steady hope for what today can find.

A road back to all that we once knew?
Maybe, or not. Certainly, though, to a better view.

"What happens next?" It's as good as gold
For those who would see God is in control.

To Plant a Tree

I saw something worse than an unplanted tree: it was two trees planted too close to each other.

For the former, who can really blame, other than the standard fare of selfishness of the age?
For the latter, it's so much worse: for the carelessness of the future, estimated wrongly the needed space to accommodate certain growth in their own place.

And that's the thing that makes me stop and break a little inside — that the symbol of the tree is reduced to vanity, and hollow style; no longer a shade for future generations, but a wall from present neighbors, and sure to be mowed down as surely as it was recently planted.

The best time to plant a tree has long since been discussed and settled, but the best way to plant one is something we derisively ignored along the way, to a point where if it might be too late, we ought to still do it anyway, for who might come along after.

In a Seed

He looks so deep into hidden-most corners to find things that can be brought forth and sees what could never be exposed: neither by deepest desire nor strongest intent; neither by keenest eye for utmost talent, nor endless dollars spent.

In a seed, who could see what is written so deep? So fine upon its line, who could read its full design? Uncover what's encoded, indecipherable by human mind?

A profile so apparent, yet so hidden in plain sight. Only its author could discern what is written on its lines.

He sees even past the current position where it might find itself, to see where it could end up being, coaxed properly toward fullest expression of self; and that, not gauged by the seed itself, but by its author who knows how to place it best — position it better than anyone else.

Man's will so free, only bound to choose; we must be careful to choose well, and prefer according to our designer, rather than any appraisal of our design.

Seeds are not made for themselves, but for those children it would expel, and even that, only once made mature in its time. (There is no promise of future, but potential for it is never more greatly seen than in a seed.)

What about choice, though?

They're made, then reinvested, and the path so carved forward toward a future so made.

But the deepest expression that could be displayed? Rarely does a seed reach that stature or esteem; often just left in the realm of a dream, never seen.

Self anchored to self is a blind man's gamble.

Self anchored to God ensures the road most stable, and toward fullest future, and that as sure as the potential in a seed.

First Frontiers

In the space just so newly defined, yet to be refined, struggling to
gain height.
A sapling, vulnerable and bare, yet sheltered by where it came
to be grown.
"How could it ever just survive, seeing all the things around it
stomp around?"
Yet what is plain to see for those who would try to see, is that it
can do nothing but grow from where it had been planted.
Though there are hazards, its destiny is sure. Its position is right. Its
aim is the sky.
And some might dare to accuse and say "if not this, then the next
thing would be. Then you would say the next was meant to be."
But observe it so close, and look at its stem. Look at its shoots.
Look at its leaves.
It is meant to be. Destined to fill the area, and see others blotted
out by the shadow it will cast.
Not another. This one.
This is the sapling of first frontiers.
It guides the way for the coming years.
And it can do no other, it is destined to be.

Even

Even the weakest of structures serves its purpose till the end
And its end, who can know it?
Who should hasten it?
Who could despise the former thing, nourished to bring them
forth?
Even in its weakest time, as a shell of what it once was, it stands.
And its stand means it merits observance.
In its weakest time, it declares it once stood strong.
And its stand commands respect.

The fool cannot see how it fits into today.
The fool will rush in to kill and destroy the thing it must despise,
despising the past and its former way.
The fool sees a new road where the old thing persists.
The fool won't yet fall in his folly, but in these modern times, be
upheld to do his bad will.

And even when the structure falls, and no one is around to hear...
the gears of time will register.
the winds of change catch hint.
the people will walk a new road forward to a place where it all
shall end.

And in the age to come shall come forth structures so permanent
and immovable
And nothing shall be destroyed or broken or razed.

And all will be made even in the great scales of justice:
boundaries reclaimed, redrawn, renamed.

A Well-Thinned Forest

Seeing that well-thinned forest with all that old growth standing
so tall
Erect against the backdrop of every good thing going by,
undisturbed and vibrant.

Cleared and clean of all underbrush — so thickened and wild
and eliminous, born to die; its fate sealed by the mere fact that a
tree's seed was sown long before, right nearby.

Nothing wrong here, as walking path is so clear, and the canopy
keeps away harsh light from hiker's head.

And all that while growing even more what already looms high
overhead.

Who Can?

Failure to launch from low place to one higher
Desperate to find wingful strength to rely on.
Who can make it all the way, all the way up the height of this
tree?
And see a view from rarer place, where there simply aren't
many?

Failure so sure, so certain, it's known
All around, of the one who couldn't climb up from home.
But stayed somewhere low, and so close to his source.
Didn't develop those wings, barely lapped 'round the course.

And the course being strong, stable, sturdy, and low.
Gave no real occasion to pace greater than slow.

And the watch stands a witness, and the peers all around
Of his weak show of ambition, of his dragging the ground

Who can meet the standard? Who can dare to take flight?
Such a day of wayward winds, and harsh sun rays, and blinding
light?

But there's a lion in the streets, such a sluggard better beware.
There's danger down here, like there's danger up there.

The reasons abound and there's trouble to be found, for any poor
soul who dares to put feet to ground, or wings to air, or really just
do anything outside of the comfort of home's staid air.

Who can make it move? Make it lift? Make it float?
Who can make it last till it all wraps up on some final day
When wild winds charge and crash the mighty tree
Once aspired to attain to, to see.

Beyond the Line of Comfort

It's the space I now occupy, the line beyond where I find
A lack of the thing so stable that keeps me safe inside

And I can't reach around, no place around to be found
Where I might feel safe now on this ground.

I'm beyond the line of comfort
Head swimming in a sick sea of sorrowful worry
Heart sinking like a stone in a hurry
A race to the bottom
Yet no bottom to be found
No sound all around.
No echoes or signs of a chamber wall now.

Just the pitch-piercing blackness of confusion
And the heart-draining steel of sorrow
Quieting all functions to the common low hum
A silencing drum, fading to zero.
Decrementing to null.

But like the seed that falls into life-giving earth
It all must die to give forth new birth.

It all must die to give forth new birth.
My only hope amidst the storm, amidst the flood, amidst the mud
That now encases my tear-strained eyes, long since dried by long
passage of time
Where I have waited, time and again for new day's dawn and
old day's end.

Watched many suns and many moons again.
Waiting for the new day that brings my ship in.
Waiting for the new day to bring warmth back within.

And I can't lie, I'm still waiting on that crack to appear, either in the soil, or in the seed, or in my fear.

Let my hope, Lord, be made whole.
Let me not be put to shame; don't leave me where I've now grown cold, as I've waited for the warmth to make me to grow.
Let me not be disqualified; I've only gotten this far by steady stride.

Don't cast me now away, when I've come so far, but now wasting away, beyond the line of comfort.

Rise and Run

Part 1: Rise

Which one did I find when I looked inside?
Rise or run, which one was the one?

To rise for me was a great place to be —
Escalation alight to a place that is bright.

And for me to run was not as fun —
To trod along to an old, known song.

Aleash I would be, bound to my feet
Unable to see something new to me.

Unchained for flight, truly my delight
To rise is so much better; to run, just no mettle

Let me see new. Let me be free.
Let me see now. Let me be me.

Part 2: Run

To elevate one's eyes to a place hidden away,
A storehouse in the heavenlies where angels stay.

To see it so clean and so bright and so true
To see all the things that you had hoped were true.
To see all the wonders that never will cease
And to be at rest fully, found in His peace.

Knowledge is peace when it comes down to man.
Knowledge is full when it falls from His hand.
Knowledge is golden when from Him it flows.
Knowledge above that nobody has known.

Asserting and climbing and gaining yet still.
No surroundings familiar yet still there's a thrill.
And heights pass me by as I climb higher still.
To a new place of wonder, to that higher thrill.

I've risen and pondered and gained a new know,
But still, I do climb to a place I don't know.
Now knowledge has weight as I feel it right now.
But how can I move with a mountain embrowed?

To run may be better now that I do see.
To run is much lighter than where I have been.
To run carries nothing but itself in the now.
To run as I rise, is that possible now?

A Journey's Worth of Growth

Tales spin light, from deepest places of human desire for well-formed future.
Soul reaches forth to touch farthest corners, straining the light of guiding intention, to find the anchor and hook in tight.
There's a long line you've drawn from where you're at to where you'd go, and many, many points and plots to fill right in to get to where you'd go.

Writing a whole journey's worth of growth? Take it all just a bit more slow. Do like they say, when they say, "steady as she goes".

"So fast! So soon!" (by implication, so tragic) "You've fallen hip-deep into the mire!"
Journey quickly stopped and halted, energy fleeting, getting tired.

This business gets all so real, from the outside looking in, so easy to map out its feel, only to be smacked so strong by the pressing on, and as soon as one enters in.

That destination, I laugh derisively at my own ignorance and at my own arrogance and at my own folly.

To think I had some large and great step to make, to call it all forth, line it up, sort it out, and infuse great warmth of light and power across all I would encounter.

A journey's worth of growth, not to say a journey's worth of journeying. I'm just not that arrogant any longer.

Unknown Lands Appearing

As distant the haze of forgotten old days
So is the vision ahead
Unknown futures rise and fall in a line
Nobody can know what is next.

But then I recall what I read on the page
Of prophecy of old John did write

How every wrong will be made right.
How every knee will bow in His sight.
How He will make all things new
And create unknown lands to be known

And there is no occasion for worry in how it might be
The very reason the present is so calm to me
Though the fig tree is shaking its fruit too early
And the sky is rolling up like a scroll to be stored
Or even replaced with something new

Unknown new skies soon will be above — ahead it's all better,
yet to be seen!
But this is the place I am heading, into unknown lands soon to
appear.

Bonus Poems

instagram

Rare Creatures of the Deep

Part 1:

They stay hidden until their unknown rule compels them to the
surface.
Stay in the corner of the corner, so much out of the way to rarely
be seen.
And even rarer still to be seen for what they are.
Driven to the depths by the hostile-but-weak
that drove them down beneath the deep.
Able to survive the strange elements so turned.
Not their native land where they sleep.
Yet they sleep...

As we slumber high above unknown realms.
The rare creature of the deep moves and turns according to its
nature so constrained to deeper depths.
Levels of survival only so known for their greater capacity to exist
all alone... as a rare creature of the deep.

Still many doubt whether it could ever be.
Nothing so described has ever been seen.
If it's ever been seen, just as quickly disproved.
Just as quickly denounced as a lunatic's ruse
To turn mystery into profit for the easily fooled.

Part 2:

But mystery remains in a world so displayed.
All things laid out, they're fully flayed.
All the viscera open and described and named.
"There's nothing left to say", they say.

And to question the reach of their exhaustive finds
And to suggest there are others yet to be described
And to lay claim to the knowledge of creatures so rare
Brings a scowl to those whose calloused hands remain bare.

"How audacious and reckless and deluded must be... to say there
is something left deep in the sea... beneath weighty depths where
the pressures press and pry... where darkness pushes strong,
breaks, and enters inside."

There is yet mystery in this world.

And for all of their searching, they've found nothing still.
And contend to accuse the one who holds up strong hope
To discover and appreciate those rare creatures of the deep.

THE MASTER PIECE

The world a broken puzzle, and all the people, its broken pieces.
The claims to which we keep on clinging defy all reason.
We've thrown away all the blueprints, made our own new
designs.
Thrown away all conventions, in favor of the fashion of our fetid
finds...
Which allow all restraint to be thrown to the side
endless vain pursuits, in which we might ever hide.
And eventually be lost, and forever remain.

Yet there is an occasion to look up to find help — an occasion to
cry out for God.
There remains a good reason to knock loud at those gates — to
seek counsel from where no man has trod.
"Who will ascend?" that's to say, "to bring Him down?"
"Never has it been, and never could it be, that one could climb
above, to descend and set us free."

Yet there is an occasion to look down for our shame — an
occasion to cry out for redemption.
There remains a good reason to bend down the knees — to seek
forgiveness, full show of contrition.
"Who will descend?" that's to say, "to bring Him up?"
"Never has it been, and never could it be, that one could go
down, to rise again and make us free."

And we say such things at the height of all folly.
Who could know the depths of God's mind or His infinite bounty
of wisdom?
We would quickly plummet down below, never again to have an
occasion to know, the goodness of what He would show, to those
who cede Him control.

Yes, we say such things from our depth of brokenness — not
knowing the fulness of His plan to fix what we mixed and
destroyed in our tortuous / twisted toil.
We would fashion in our image a ladder made only of rope,

formed of the folly of our flaccid hope. Can it be climbed? The answer is "nope".

So, whose name can we claim, fit for the purpose of our Age.
Promised once, and so, proclaimed
to be the King, born of man, to reign?

The Master Piece is His name, and He has so many other:
King of Kings, Lord of Lords, Alpha and Omega...
The One who is whole, and who's never not been...
The One who is perfect, wholly without sin...
The One who is pure, full of power to do...
All of His intention, show His promises sure.

God's first intention in the person of His Son
Eternally co-existent, Trinity: Godhead. three-in-one.

Pre-set to descend, be born, live, love, and then die.
And pre-set to ascend, on the third day to rise.

And for there to ever be...
Awaiting the day to set us free...
turn over, finally, this tapestry...
of a puzzle turned upside down...
and all be made right again.

The missing piece proven masterful throughout.
Fixed the broken puzzle, and its pieces
and the table where it was all laid out!

God's final solution, yet so sure from the very start.
The person of Jesus Christ, image of the Father's heart.

Black and White Days

"In the haze of past days, yeah, there was fortune to be seen... and to be held! That, I beheld, and nothing else, in those black and white days."

*"Summers never ended, and Winters never ceased.
Hardships never let up, and good times always pleased."*

See, everything is so jumbled and confused when viewing the deepest of hindsight!
What benefit can be gathered from such dimness of light?

(The past always fading, no strength for the fight. And history seems a lie, no fruitful gain in sight.)

Well, that's exactly where I found myself — in the quiet and still deep pond. Staring into the rich and darkening depths of what once was, and still is down below. Still coursing and crafting what remains above, and continues to grow (yes, them both)

In the turn of a moment, that's where I found myself — deep in the black and the white.
Coursing to discern the pattern and sort it all out, and find both the reason and the rhyme.

To identify the rhythm / To course it within
To move it so slightly / To change what it sends

Out into the world! Once again, to be seen!
Not the black and white pattern, but colors diffused from now-brightest beam!

It was all from deep in the black and the white
that the new thing came forth, produced from old light...

And itself weathering still too, what has come forth from that to one day still speak of Colorful Days in the same vein of fact as black and white days.

Neologisms (developed by author)

Aleash. *adjective.* bound to a leash; leashed, tethered.

Colorflows. *noun.* Just as the sky has its clouds and rainbows, I imagined colorflows as a kind of ground rainbow, laying much like fog would over a field, but with the brilliance, splendor, and clarity of a rainbow.

Eliminous. *adjective.* Having the quality of temporariness, made to be destroyed.

Embrowed. *adjective.* Weighing upon someone's brow, figuratively. A burden that would coax distress and concern.

Sollow. *adjective.* portmanteau of "sad" and "hollow", meaning sadness due to being hollow. Also supposed to invoke both of its word neighbors: "sallow" (meaning sickly appearing), and "sorrow" (indicating a deep sadness).

Sollowful. *adjective.* magnify the imagery of 'sollow'; that such a person is full of a hollowness that is to be lamented for what they will miss due to their deficiency.

Staid. *adjective.* **Derived from English verb "to stay".** Placed somewhere to remain there. To invoke the comfort of a thing being where it is expected.

Staity. *noun.* the state of being placed, to be found where expected.

Wall-testing. *gerund.* Probing the strength of one's peripheral constraints in order to identify possibility for changing direction, despite there being no apparent path.

Wingful. *adjective.* Manifesting traits inherent to a wing's abilities.

From the author:

Thank you for purchasing this book and spending your time reading through these poems. I hope you have enjoyed them, and worked through them thoughtfully and carefully. I also hope you have a favorite or two (or more) that you might even revisit. My deepest hope is that something you've read here has sparked to life a fresh vein of wonder within you.

My goal with this collection was to present a fairly tight work, adequate to the task of building a strong picture of how things change, while also providing enough variety to enjoy the journey toward that view.

Please be on the lookout for my new collections in the future. There are currently 3 other collections I want to bring to print at the time of this first printing of *How Things Change* (November 2022).

I thank Book Mobile for their incredible work and end product, seen in the printing and binding of this collection.

Finally, I do want to be very explicit here in giving all honor and glory to God and to the Lord Jesus Christ who has saved me from my sins. To Him be all honor and glory, forever and ever. His Kingdom come and His Will be done on earth as it is in Heaven. Amen.

—Ronnie Barnes
November 15th, 2022